JOURNEYS

Practice Book
Volume 1
Kindergarten

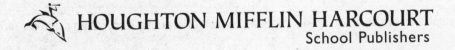

HOUGHTON MIFFLIN HARCOURT
School Publishers

Contents

Contents

Name _____

Aa Bb Cc Dd Ee Ff Gg Hh Ii Jj Kk Ll Mm

Nn Oo Pp Qq Rr Ss Tt Uu Vv Ww Xx Yy Zz

A a A a

M x A b S a F I
r A a C a T n A
O z L a A i A a
a J a A h A A a

Directions Have children identify and write uppercase *A* and lowercase *a*. Then have them circle all the *A*'s and *a*'s in the box.

Remind children to write the upper- and lowercase letters so they can be easily read, using a left-to-right and top-to-bottom progression.

Letter Names

Kindergarten, Welcome to Kindergarten

Name _____

Aa Bb Cc Dd Ee Ff Gg Hh Ii Jj Kk Ll Mm

Nn Oo Pp Qq Rr Ss Tt Uu Vv Ww Xx Yy Zz

Bb Bb

B	y	B	c	T	b	G	m
s	B	b	D	b	U	o	B
P	a	M	b	B	j	B	a
S	K	b	C	i	M	B	b

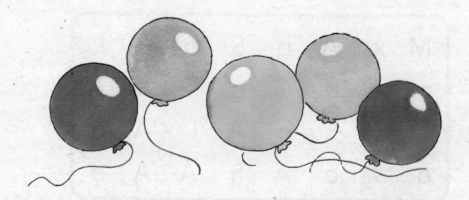

Directions Have children identify and write uppercase *B* and lowercase *b*. Then have them circle all the *B*'s and *b*'s in the box.

Remind children to write the upper- and lowercase letters so they can be easily read, using a left-to-right and top-to-bottom progression.

Name _____

Aa Bb Cc Dd Ee Ff Gg Hh Ii Jj Kk Ll Mm

Nn Oo Pp Qq Rr Ss Tt Uu Vv Ww Xx Yy Zz

Cc Cc _____

O	z	C	d	U	c	H	n
t	H	c	E	c	V	p	C
Q	b	N	c	C	k	C	c
a	L	c	C	j	C	C	M

Directions Have children identify and write uppercase *C* and lowercase *c*. Then have them circle all the *C*'s and *c*'s in the box.

Remind children to write the upper- and lowercase letters so they can be easily read, using a left-to-right and top-to-bottom progression.

Name _____

Aa Bb Cc Dd Ee Ff Gg Hh Ii Jj Kk Ll Mm

Nn Oo Pp Qq Rr Ss Tt Uu Vv Ww Xx Yy Zz

Dd D̶d̶

P	a	D	e	V	d	I	o
u	D	d	F	d	W	q	D
R	c	O	d	D	l	D	d
d	M	d	D	k	D	D	d

Directions Have children identify and write uppercase *D* and lowercase *d*. Then have them circle all the *D*'s and *d*'s in the box.

Remind children to write the upper- and lowercase letters so they can be easily read, using a left-to-right and top-to-bottom progression.

Name _____

Aa Bb Cc Dd Ee Ff Gg Hh Ii Jj Kk Ll Mm

Nn Oo Pp Qq Rr Ss Tt Uu Vv Ww Xx Yy Zz

 Ee Ee

E	b	E	f	W	a	J	x
v	E	e	G	e	X	r	E
S	d	P	e	E	m	E	e
r	N	e	E	l	H	E	e

Directions Have children identify and write uppercase *E* and lowercase *e*. Then have them circle all the *E*'s and *e*'s in the box.

Remind children to write the upper- and lowercase letters so they can be easily read, using a left-to-right and top-to-bottom progression.

Letter Names

Kindergarten, Welcome to Kindergarten

Name _____

Aa Bb Cc Dd Ee Ff Gg Hh Ii Jj Kk Ll Mm

Nn Oo Pp Qq Rr Ss Tt Uu Vv Ww Xx Yy Zz

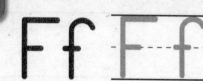

Ff Ff

R	c	F	g	X	f	K	q
w	F	f	H	f	Y	s	F
T	e	Q	f	F	n	F	f
f	O	f	F	m	F	F	f

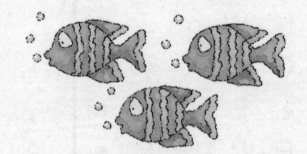

Directions Have children identify and write uppercase *F* and lowercase *f*. Then have them circle all the *F*'s and *f*'s in the box.

Remind children to write the upper- and lowercase letters so they can be easily read, using a left-to-right and top-to-bottom progression.

Name _____

Aa Bb Cc Dd Ee Ff Gg Hh Ii Jj Kk Ll Mm

Nn Oo Pp Qq Rr Ss Tt Uu Vv Ww Xx Yy Zz

Gg Gg

S	d	V	h	Y	g	L	r
x	G	g	I	g	Z	t	B
U	f	R	g	G	o	G	g
b	P	g	T	s	G	G	g

Directions Have children identify and write uppercase *G* and lowercase *g*. Then have them circle all the *G*'s and *g*'s in the box.

Remind children to write the upper- and lowercase letters so they can be easily read, using a left-to-right and top-to-bottom progression.

Letter Names

Kindergarten, Welcome to Kindergarten

Name _____

Aa Bb Cc Dd Ee Ff Gg Hh Ii Jj Kk Ll Mm

Nn Oo Pp Qq Rr Ss Tt Uu Vv Ww Xx Yy Zz

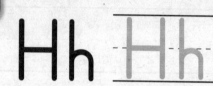

Hh Hh

T	e	H	i	Z	h	M	s
y	H	H	J	h	A	U	H
V	g	S	h	H	P	H	h
h	Q	h	H	o	H	H	h

Directions Have children identify and write uppercase *H* and lowercase *h*. Then have them circle all the *H*'s and *h*'s in the box.

Remind children to write the upper- and lowercase letters so they can be easily read, using a left-to-right and top-to-bottom progression.

Name _____

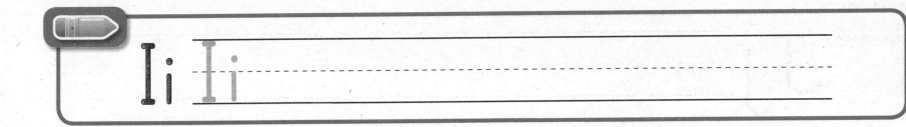

Aa Bb Cc Dd Ee Ff Gg Hh Ii Jj Kk Ll Mm

Nn Oo Pp Qq Rr Ss Tt Uu Vv Ww Xx Yy Zz

I i   I i

U	n	I	j	I	i	N	t
z	I	i	K	i	B	v	I
L	h	T	i	I	q	I	d
a	R	i	H	p	I	C	i

Directions Have children identify and write uppercase *I* and lowercase *i*. Then have them circle all the *I*'s and *i*'s in the box.

Remind children to write the upper- and lowercase letters so they can be easily read, using a left-to-right and top-to-bottom progression.

Name _____

Aa Bb Cc Dd Ee Ff Gg Hh Ii Jj Kk Ll Mm

Nn Oo Pp Qq Rr Ss Tt Uu Vv Ww Xx Yy Zz

J j J j _____

V	g	J	k	B	j	O	u
a	J	j	L	j	C	w	J
X	i	U	J	j	r	J	j
j	S	j	J	p	J	J	j

Directions Have children identify and write uppercase *J* and lowercase *j*. Then have them circle all the *J*'s and *j*'s in the box.

Remind children to write the upper- and lowercase letters so they can be easily read, using a left-to-right and top-to-bottom progression.

Letter Names

Kindergarten, Welcome to Kindergarten

Name _____

Aa Bb Cc Dd Ee Ff Gg Hh Ii Jj Kk Ll Mm

Nn Oo Pp Qq Rr Ss Tt Uu Vv Ww Xx Yy Zz

Kk

W	h	K	l	C	k	P	v
b	K	k	M	k	E	x	K
Y	j	V	k	K	s	K	k
k	T	k	K	q	K	K	k

Directions Have children identify and write uppercase *K* and lowercase *k*. Then have them circle all the *K*'s and *k*'s in the box.

Remind children to write the upper- and lowercase letters so they can be easily read, using a left-to-right and top-to-bottom progression.

1

Lesson 1
PRACTICE BOOK

What Makes a Family?
Words to Know: I

Name _____

I

1. _____ .

2. _____ .

3. _____ .

Directions Have children look at each picture and name the action. Then have them write the word *I* to complete each sentence. Have children read the completed sentences aloud.

Have children clap once for each word as they read the sentences aloud again. Have children say other sentences with the word *I*.

Words to Know

Kindergarten, Unit 1: Friendly Faces

Name _____

Aa Bb Cc Dd Ee Ff Gg Hh Ii Jj Kk Ll Mm

Nn Oo Pp Qq Rr Ss Tt Uu Vv Ww Xx Yy Zz

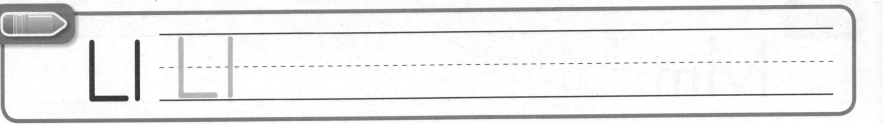

Ll

X	i	L	m	D	l	Q	w
c	L	l	N	l	F	y	L
Z	k	W	l	L	t	L	l
l	U	l	L	r	L	L	l

Directions Have children identify and write uppercase *L* and lowercase *l*. Then have them circle all the *L*'s and *l*'s in the box.

Remind children to write the upper- and lowercase letters so they can be easily read, using a left-to-right and top-to-bottom progression.

Name _____

Aa Bb Cc Dd Ee Ff Gg Hh Ii Jj Kk Ll Mm

Nn Oo Pp Qq Rr Ss Tt Uu Vv Ww Xx Yy Zz

Mm Mm

Y	j	B	n	M	m	R	x
d	M	m	O	m	G	z	L
A	l	X	m	M	u	D	m
g	V	m	M	s	e	M	m

Directions Have children identify and write uppercase *M* and lowercase *m*. Then have them circle all the *M*'s and *m*'s in the box.

Remind children to write the upper- and lowercase letters so they can be easily read, using a left-to-right and top-to-bottom progression.

Name _____

Main Ideas

Directions Tell children to draw a picture to show some important facts they learned about families in the selection. Have children share their pictures with the class. Tell them to speak clearly and use complete sentences as they share their information. In addition, tell them to listen carefully and face others as they share.

Comprehension

Kindergarten, Unit 1: Friendly Faces

Name _____

Aa Bb Cc Dd Ee Ff Gg Hh Ii Jj Kk Ll Mm

Nn Oo Pp Qq Rr Ss Tt Uu Vv Ww Xx Yy Zz

N n Nn

Z	k	N	o	F	n	S	y
e	N	n	P	n	H	a	N
B	m	Y	n	N	v	N	n
n	W	n	N	t	N	N	n

Directions Have children identify and write uppercase *N* and lowercase *n*. Then have them circle all the *N*'s and *n*'s in the box.

Remind children to write the upper- and lowercase letters so they can be easily read, using a left-to-right and top-to-bottom progression.

Letter Names

Kindergarten, Unit 1: Friendly Faces

Name _____

Aa Bb Cc Dd Ee Ff Gg Hh Ii Jj Kk Ll Mm

Nn Oo Pp Qq Rr Ss Tt Uu Vv Ww Xx Yy Zz

A	l	H	o	G	p	T	z
d	O	o	Q	h	I	b	T
C	n	Z	o	O	w	O	o
o	X	o	O	u	A	O	b

Directions Have children identify and write uppercase *O* and lowercase *o*. Then have them circle all the *O*'s and *o*'s in the box.

Remind children to write the upper- and lowercase letters so they can be easily read, using a left-to-right and top-to-bottom progression.

7

Letter Names

Name _____

Nouns for People

1.

2.

3.

Directions Have children look at the first row of pictures and underline the mother. Have them look at the second row and underline the father. Then have them look at the third one and underline the grandmother. Then have children identify the pictures of the grown-ups and draw a circle around them. Tell children to draw a picture in the box of someone in their family. Have them label their picture and then tell about it.

Grammar

8

Kindergarten, Unit 1: Friendly Faces

Name _____

Aa Bb Cc Dd Ee Ff Gg Hh Ii Jj Kk Ll Mm

Nn Oo Pp Qq Rr Ss Tt Uu Vv Ww Xx Yy Zz

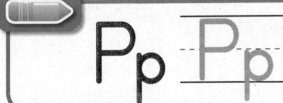

Pp Pp

B	m	P	p	H	q	U	a
g	P	P	R	p	J	c	P
D	o	A	p	P	x	P	p
p	Y	p	P	v	P	P	p

Directions Have children identify and write uppercase *P* and lowercase *p*. Then have them circle all the *P*'s and *p*'s in the box.

Remind children to write the upper- and lowercase letters so they can be easily read, using a left-to-right and top-to-bottom progression.

Letter Names

Kindergarten, Unit 1: Friendly Faces

like

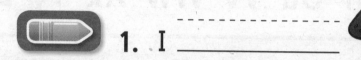

1. I _____

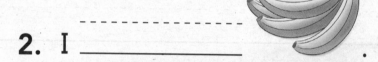

2. I _____

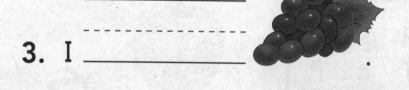

3. I _____

4. I _____

Directions Have children read the word *I* and name each picture. Then have them write the word *like* to complete each sentence. Have children read the completed sentences aloud.

Have children point to and say the names of letters they recognize on the page. Then have children clap once for each word as they read the sentences aloud again. Have children say other sentences with the word *like*.

Words to Know

Kindergarten, Unit 1: Friendly Faces

Name _____

Aa Bb Cc Dd Ee Ff Gg Hh Ii Jj Kk Ll Mm

Nn Oo Pp Qq Rr Ss Tt Uu Vv Ww Xx Yy Zz

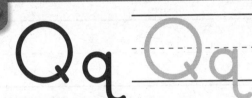

Qq Qq

C	n	Q	q	I	r	V	b
Q	Q	q	S	q	K	d	Q
E	p	B	q	Q	y	K	s
q	Z	m	Q	w	J	Q	q

Directions Have children identify and write uppercase *Q* and lowercase *q*. Then have them circle all the *Q*'s and *q*'s in the box.

Remind children to write the upper- and lowercase letters so they can be easily read, using a left-to-right and top-to-bottom progression.

Lesson 2
PRACTICE BOOK

How Do Dinosaurs Go to School?
Letter Names: Letter *Rr*

Name _____

Aa Bb Cc Dd Ee Ff Gg Hh Ii Jj Kk Ll Mm

Nn Oo Pp Qq Rr Ss Tt Uu Vv Ww Xx Yy Zz

Rr   Rr

D	o	R	r	J	s	W	c
i	R	r	T	r	L	e	R
F	q	C	r	R	z	R	r
r	A	r	R	x	R	R	r

Directions Have children identify and write uppercase *R* and lowercase *r*. Then have them circle all the *R*'s and *r*'s in the box.

Remind children to write the upper- and lowercase letters so they can be easily read, using a left-to-right and top-to-bottom progression.

12

Name _____

Understanding Characters

Directions Tell children to draw a picture that shows how their favorite character feels in the story. Then have them draw a picture to show how they would feel if they were in a classroom with a dinosaur.

Have children share their pictures and talk about each one. Tell them to speak clearly and use complete sentences as they share their ideas.

Comprehension

13

Kindergarten, Unit 1: Friendly Faces

Name _____

Aa Bb Cc Dd Ee Ff Gg Hh Ii Jj Kk Ll Mm

Nn Oo Pp Qq Rr Ss Tt Uu Vv Ww Xx Yy Zz

S s   S s

E	p	S	s	K	t	s	d
j	S	s	U	G	M	f	S
G	r	D	s	S	a	S	o
h	B	s	Q	y	S	S	s

Directions Have children identify and write uppercase *S* and lowercase *s*. Then have them circle all the *S*'s and *s*'s in the box.

Remind children to write the upper- and lowercase letters so they can be easily read, using a left-to-right and top-to-bottom progression.

Name _____

Aa Bb Cc Dd Ee Ff Gg Hh Ii Jj Kk Ll Mm

Nn Oo Pp Qq Rr Ss Tt Uu Vv Ww Xx Yy Zz

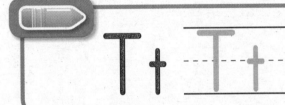

Tt Tt

F	q	T	t	L	u	Y	e
j	T	t	V	t	N	g	T
H	s	E	t	T	b	T	t
t	C	t	T	z	T	T	t

Directions Have children identify and write uppercase *T* and lowercase *t*. Then have them circle all the *T*'s and *t*'s in the box.

Remind children to write the upper- and lowercase letters so they can be easily read, using a left-to-right and top-to-bottom progression.

Letter Names

15

Kindergarten, Unit 1: Friendly Faces

Name _____

Nouns for Places

1.

2.

3.

Directions Have children name the pictures in the first row. Have them underline the picture that shows a place. Repeat for the second and third rows.

Then have children draw a picture of a favorite place in the box. Have them label their picture and then tell about it.

Name _____

Aa Bb Cc Dd Ee Ff Gg Hh Ii Jj Kk Ll Mm

Nn Oo Pp Qq Rr Ss Tt Uu Vv Ww Xx Yy Zz

Uu Uu

G	r	U	r	M	v	Z	f
k	U	u	W	p	O	h	U
I	t	F	u	U	c	U	d
A	D	u	B	a	U	Y	u

Directions Have children identify and write uppercase *U* and lowercase *u*. Then have them circle all the *U*'s and *u*'s in the box.

Remind children to write the upper- and lowercase letters so they can be easily read, using a left-to-right and top-to-bottom progression.

Letter Names

Kindergarten, Unit 1: Friendly Faces

Name _____

the

1. I like _____  .

2. I like _____  .

3. I like _____ .

Directions Have children read the words *I like* and name each picture. Then have them write the word *the* to complete each sentence. Have children read the completed sentences aloud.

Have children point to and say the names of letters they recognize on the page. Then have children clap once for each word as they read the sentences aloud again. Have children say other sentences with the word *the*.

Words to Know

18

Kindergarten, Unit 1: Friendly Faces

Name _____

Aa Bb Cc Dd Ee Ff Gg Hh Ii Jj Kk Ll Mm

Nn Oo Pp Qq Rr Ss Tt Uu Vv Ww Xx Yy Zz

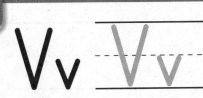

Vv

H	s	V	v	N	w	A	f
I	V	v	X	v	P	i	V
J	u	G	V	V	d	V	v
v	E	v	V	b	V	V	v

Directions Have children identify and write uppercase *V* and lowercase *v*. Then have them circle all the *V*'s and *v*'s in the box.

Remind children to write the upper- and lowercase letters so they can be easily read, using a left-to-right and top-to-bottom progression.

Kindergarten, Unit 1: Friendly Faces

Name _____

Aa Bb Cc Dd Ee Ff Gg Hh Ii Jj Kk Ll Mm

Nn Oo Pp Qq Rr Ss Tt Uu Vv Ww Xx Yy Zz

Ww Ww

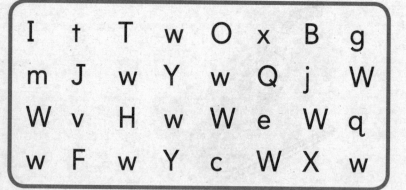

I	t	T	w	O	x	B	g
m	J	w	Y	w	Q	j	W
W	v	H	w	W	e	W	q
w	F	w	Y	c	W	X	w

Directions Have children identify and write uppercase *W* and lowercase *w*. Then have them circle all the *W*'s and *w*'s in the box.

Remind children to write the upper- and lowercase letters so they can be easily read, using a left-to-right and top-to-bottom progression.

Letter Names

20

Kindergarten, Unit 1: Friendly Faces

Name _____

Story Structure

Directions Tell children to draw a picture of the main character from the story. Have them show the setting in the background. Then have them draw a picture to show their favorite event in the story. Have children share their pictures. Have them use location words, such as *above* or *below* to describe parts of their pictures. Then have them retell or act out the key event they illustrated.

21

Comprehension

Kindergarten, Unit 1: Friendly Faces

Name _____

Aa Bb Cc Dd Ee Ff Gg Hh Ii Jj Kk Ll Mm

Nn Oo Pp Qq Rr Ss Tt Uu Vv Ww Xx Yy Zz

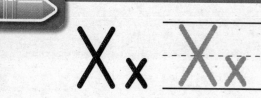

Xx Xx

J	u	X	x	P	y	C	h
n	X	x	Z	x	R	k	X
L	w	I	x	X	f	X	x
x	G	x	X	d	X	X	x

Directions Have children identify and write uppercase *X* and lowercase *x*. Then have them circle all the *X*'s and *x*'s in the box.

Remind children to write the upper- and lowercase letters so they can be easily read, using a left-to-right and top-to-bottom progression.

Kindergarten, Unit 1: Friendly Faces

Name _____

| | | | | | | | | | | | | |
Aa Bb Cc Dd Ee Ff Gg Hh Ii Jj Kk Ll Mm

Nn Oo Pp Qq Rr Ss Tt Uu Vv Ww Xx Yy Zz

Yy Yy

K	v	G	y	Q	z	D	i
o	E	y	A	y	S	l	Y
M	x	J	y	Y	g	Y	y
n	H	y	F	e	Y	Z	D

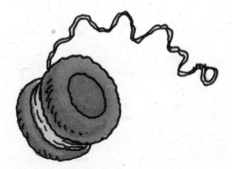

Name _____

Aa Bb Cc Dd Ee Ff Gg Hh Ii Jj Kk Ll Mm

Nn Oo Pp Qq Rr Ss Tt Uu Vv Ww Xx Yy Zz

Zz Zz

L	w	Z	z	R	a	E	j
p	Z	z	B	z	T	m	Z
N	y	K	z	Z	h	Z	z
z	I	z	Z	f	Z	Z	z

Directions Have children identify and write uppercase Z and lowercase z. Then have them circle all the Z's and z's in the box.

Remind children to write the upper- and lowercase letters so they can be easily read, using a left-to-right and top-to-bottom progression.

Name _____

Nouns for Animals and Things

1.

2.

3.

Directions Have children name the pictures in the first row. Have them tell whether each picture shows an animal or a thing. Have them underline the picture that shows an animal and draw a circle around the picture that shows a thing.

Repeat for the second and third rows. Then have children draw a picture in the box of a favorite animal or thing. Have them dictate or write a caption for their picture.

Grammar

25

Kindergarten, Unit 1: Friendly Faces

Name ____________________

and

1. I like  ________  .

2. I like  ________ 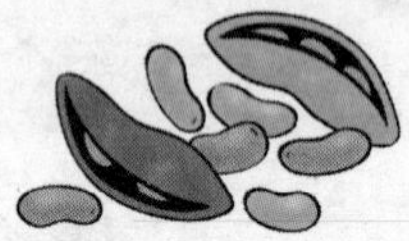 .

3. I like  ________  .

4. I like  ________ 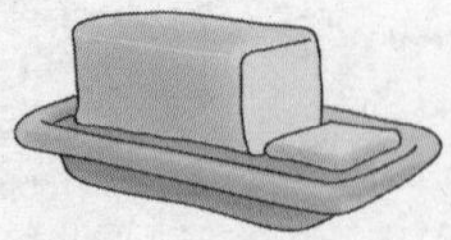 .

Directions Have children read the words *I like* and name each picture. Then have them write the word *and* to complete each sentence. Have children read the completed sentences aloud.

Have children point to and say the names of letters they recognize on the page. Then have children clap once for each word as they read the sentences aloud again. Have children say other sentences with the word *and*.

Name _____

1.   **Mm** M m _____  _____

2.

 _____

 _____

 _____

 _____

 _____

 _____

Directions Have children name the Alphafriend and its letter. Have them trace and write *M* and *m*. Then have them write *Mm* next to the pictures whose names start with the /m/ sound.

Help children think of groups of words that begin with the /m/ sound. For example, *My monkey moves more.*

Name _____

1.  Mm   Mm

2.

Directions Have children name the Alphafriend and its letter. Have them trace and write *Mm*. Remind children to write the upper- and lowercase letters so they can be easily read, using a left-to-right and top-to-bottom progression. Then tell children to name each picture and write the letter *m* when they hear the /m/ sound.

Name

Text and Graphic Features

1.

2.

Directions Tell children to look at the first set of pictures. Have them circle the picture that best describes a man that helps children cross the street. Have children name the sign and explain why the man is holding it. Then have them look at the second set of pictures and circle the picture that best describes a girl that delivers newspapers. Discuss with children how they matched the spoken words to the correct picture. Then ask children how pictures can help them better understand information they read about.

Comprehension

Kindergarten, Unit 1: Friendly Faces

Name _____

Ask Questions

Directions Have children share questions they might have about *Everybody Works*. Encourage them to discuss the different kinds of work people do. Remind children to speak in complete sentences. Have children draw a picture of their favorite kind of work from the selection. Have children take turns explaining their choice by speaking clearly and in complete sentences.

Action Verbs in Present Tense

I like

1. I _____

2. _____

Directions Have children name each picture. Then have them complete each sentence by writing a word from the box and circling the picture that shows an action. Have children identify and act out each of the action words. Have children read their sentences aloud using an action word to describe the picture they circled. Tell them to speak clearly as they share their sentences and to listen carefully to others as they share.

Grammar

31

Kindergarten, Unit 1: Friendly Faces

Name _____

I   like   the   and

1. I _____ the  .

2. I like _____  .

3. _____ like the  .

4. I like 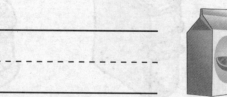 _____ .

Directions Have children read the words in the box and name each picture. Then have them write the correct word from the box to complete each sentence. Have children read the completed sentences aloud.

Have children point to and say the names of letters they recognize on the page. Then have them clap once for each word as they read the sentences aloud again. Have children tell a story using all of the Words to Know.

Words to Know

Kindergarten, Unit 1: Friendly Faces

Name _____

My Ideas

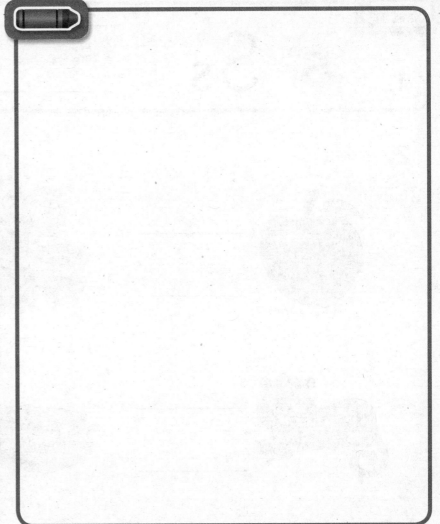

Directions Help children **generate ideas** for their writing. Have children write ideas for their class stories under *My Ideas*. Guide children to write words or draw pictures showing the characters, setting, and what will happen in their stories.

Writing

33

Kindergarten, Unit 1: Friendly Faces

Name _____

1. S s   S   s

2.

 _____

 _____

 _____

 _____

 _____

 _____

Directions Have children name the Alphafriend and its letter. Have them trace and write *Ss*. Then have them write *Ss* next to the pictures whose names start with the /s/ sound.

Help children think of groups of words that begin with the /s/ sound. For example, *Sarah says six sentences.*

Name _____

My Story

Directions Help children **develop drafts** of their writing. Encourage them to use their ideas on Practice Book page 33 as a guide in writing drafts of their stories. Remind children that they will have a chance to add more details to their stories later on in the writing process. Have children use what they know about letters and words to write their stories. Remind them to think about events in their stories and the order in which they happen. Have children begin sequencing details and actions in their stories.

Writing

Kindergarten, Unit 1: Friendly Faces

1. 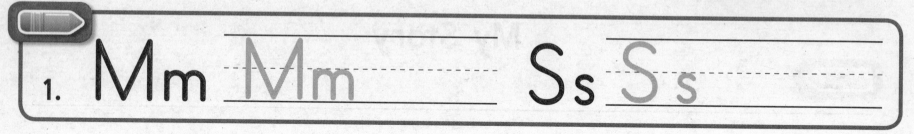 Mm Mm   Ss Ss

2.

Directions Have children name each letter. Have them write *Mm* and *Ss*. Then tell children to name the pictures and write the letter for the sound they hear at the beginning of each picture name.

Remind children to write the upper- and lowercase letters so they can be easily read, using a left-to-right and top-to-bottom progression.

Name _____

Sequence of Events

Directions Have children look at the pictures and remind them what happened at the beginning and middle of the story. Then have children draw a picture of what happens at the end of the story. Have children share their pictures and point out the key event at the end of the story. Have children use sequence words, such as *first, next,* and *last,* to retell the story. Then have children tell which words are sequence words.

Comprehension

Kindergarten, Unit 1: Friendly Faces

Name _____

My Story

Directions Help children **revise drafts** of their writing. Help them read the stories they wrote on Practice Book page 35. Talk about sentences and details they could add to make their stories even better. Help children organize their story by beginning, middle, and end. Have them write their revised stories on the lines above.

Writing

Kindergarten, Unit 1: Friendly Faces

Name _____

My Story

Directions Help children **edit drafts** of their writing. Help children read the stories they wrote on Practice Book page 38. Have them edit their drafts by writing their stories again on the lines above. Remind them to leave spaces between letters and words and to write using complete sentences. Remind them to capitalize the first letter of every sentence and end every sentence with the correct punctuation. Have children consult a picture dictionary, if necessary, for correct spelling.

Writing

Kindergarten, Unit 1: Friendly Faces

Name _____

Identify Media Forms

1.

2.

Directions Page through *Kite Flying* with children. Then have them identify and discuss the different forms of media above. Have children circle which forms they think might have more information about kites. Then have children choose their favorite media form and draw a picture of it. Have children take turns explaining their choice by speaking one at a time and in complete sentences.

Media Literacy

40

Kindergarten, Unit 1: Friendly Faces

Name _____

Action Verbs in Present Tense

I like

 1. I _____

2. _____ like

Directions Have children name each picture. Have them complete each sentence by writing a word from the box and circling the picture that shows an action.

Have children read their sentences aloud using an action word to describe the picture they circled. Tell them to speak clearly as they share their sentences and to listen carefully to others as they share.

Grammar

41

Kindergarten, Unit 1: Friendly Faces

Name _____

My Story

Directions Help children **share** their writing. Have them write final drafts of their stories on the lines above. Children may draw pictures showing the beginning, middle, and end of their stories on separate paper. Have children take turns reading aloud their stories and sharing their pictures. Guide them to explain the sequence of events. Have them identify and use sequence words such as *first, next,* and *last*. Remind children to listen attentively and to speak audibly and clearly when sharing stories.

Writing

Kindergarten, Unit 1: Friendly Faces

Name _____

---

1. I _____ the	.

2. I _____ the .

3. I _____ the .

Directions Have children read the word in the box and name each picture. Then have them write the word *see* to complete each sentence. Have children read the completed sentences aloud.

Have children point to and say the names of letters they recognize on the page. Then have children clap once for each word as they read the sentences aloud again. Have children say other sentences with the word *see*.

43

Kindergarten, Unit 2: Show and Tell

Name _____

1.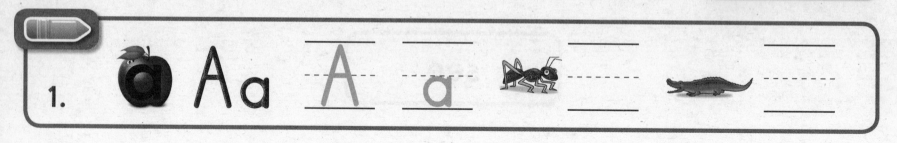

2.

Directions Have children write their name at the top of the page. Have them name the **Alphafriend** and its letter. Have children trace and write *A* and *a*. Then have them write *Aa* next to the pictures whose names start with the /a/ sound.

Help children think of groups of words that begin with the /a/ sound. For example, *attic, actor, apple*.

Phonics

44

Kindergarten, Unit 2: Show and Tell

Name _____

1. Aa _Aa_ Mm _Mm_

2.

 _____

 _____

 _____

 _____

 _____

 _____

Directions Have children write their name at the top of the page. Have them name and write *Aa* and *Mm*. Then tell children to name the pictures and write the letter for the sound they hear at the beginning of each name.

Remind children to write the upper- and lowercase letters so they can be easily read, using a left-to-right and top-to-bottom progression.

Name _____

Compare and Contrast

1. I can taste the .

3.

2. I can touch the _____ .

Comprehension

Kindergarten, Unit 2: Show and Tell

Name _____

Identify Sources

1.

2.

Directions Have children circle the best place to find how flowers look, feel, and smell. Have them identify what kinds of sources or people they could use. Then have children draw one source or person they would use. Have children take turns explaining their choice by speaking clearly and in complete sentences.

Research

Kindergarten, Unit 2: Show and Tell

Name _____

Sensory Words

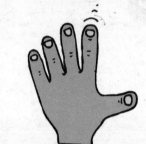   

Directions Tell children to look at and name the pictures. Have children draw a line from each sense in the top row to the picture it describes in the bottom row. Have children write a complete sentence that describes one of the pictures. Have them include sensory words in their sentences. Have them share their sentences with the class.

Grammar

48

Kindergarten, Unit 2: Show and Tell

Name _____

$$\boxed{\textbf{We}}$$

1. _____ see the .

2. _____ see the .

3. _____ see the and .

Directions Have children write their name at the top of the page. Have children read the word in the box and name each picture. Then have them write the word *We* to complete each sentence. Have children read the completed sentences aloud.

Have children point to and say the names of letters they recognize on the page. Then have children clap once for each word as they read the sentences aloud again. Have children say other sentences with the word *we*.

Words to Know

Kindergarten, Unit 2: Show and Tell

Name _____

1.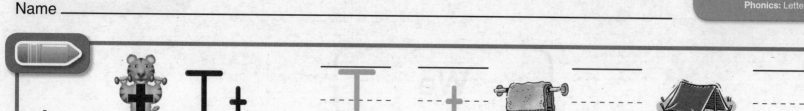

2.

Directions Have children write their name at the top of the page. Have children trace and write *T* and *t*. Then have them write *Tt* next to the pictures whose names start with the /t/ sound.

Help children think of groups of words that begin with the /t/ sound. For example, *tiger, touchdown, trumpet.*

Phonics

Kindergarten, Unit 2: Show and Tell

Name _____

1.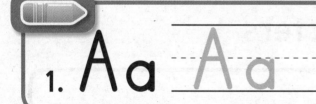

2.

 _____

  _____

 _____

 _____

 _____

 _____

Directions Have children name and write *Aa* and *Tt*. Then tell children to name the pictures and write the letter for the sound they hear at the beginning of each picture name.

Remind children to write the upper- and lowercase letters so they can be easily read, using a left-to-right and top-to-bottom progression.

Name _____

Understanding Characters

Directions Tell children to draw a picture of their favorite animal character from *Mice Squeak, We Speak*. Then have them draw a picture to show how the animal feels when it makes its sound.

Have children share their pictures. Page through the Big Book and have children name each character.

Comprehension

52

Kindergarten, Unit 2: Show and Tell

Name _____

Ask Questions

Directions Have children share questions they might have about *Mice Speak, We Squeak*. Encourage them to discuss the different sounds that animals make. Remind children to speak in complete sentences.

Have children draw a picture of their favorite animal from the selection. Have children take turns explaining their choice by speaking clearly and in complete sentences.

Research

Kindergarten, Unit 2: Show and Tell

Name _____

Sensory Words

 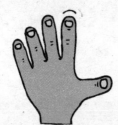   

Directions Have children name the pictures in each row. Have them draw a line from each sense in the top row to the picture it describes in the bottom row. Then have children write a complete sentence that describes one of the pictures.

Have them include sensory words in their sentences. Ask children to share their sentences with the class.

Grammar

54

Kindergarten, Unit 2: Show and Tell

Name _____

a

_____
_ _ _ _ _ _
1. I like _____ .

_____
_ _ _ _ _ _
2. I like _____ .

_____
_ _ _ _ _ _
3. We like _____ .

Directions Have children write their name at the top of the page. Have children read the word in the box and name each picture. Then have them write the word *a* to complete each sentence. Have children read the completed sentences aloud.

Have children point to and say the names of letters they recognize on the page. Then have children clap once for each word as they read the sentences aloud again. Have children say other sentences with the word *a*.

Words to Know

Kindergarten, Unit 2: Show and Tell

Name _____

1.

2.

 _____

 _____

 _____

 _____

 _____

 _____

Directions Have children write their name at the top of the page. Have them name the Alphafriend and its letter. Have children trace and write *C* and *c*. Then have them write *Cc* next to the pictures whose names start with the /k/ sound.

Help children think of groups of words that begin with the /k/ sound. For example, *cart, cupcake, cap*.

Phonics

Kindergarten, Unit 2: Show and Tell

Name _____

1.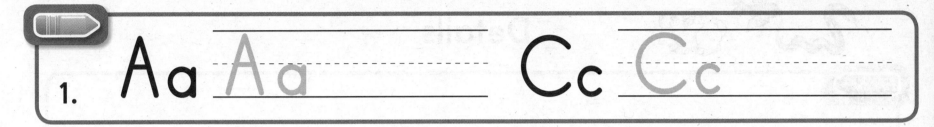

2.

Directions Have children write their name at the top of the page. Have children name and write *Aa* and *Cc*. Then tell children to name the pictures and write the letter for the sound they hear at the beginning of each picture name.

Remind children to write the upper- and lowercase letters so they can be easily read, using a left-to-right and top-to-bottom progression.

Phonics

57

Kindergarten, Unit 2: Show and Tell

Name _____

Details

Directions Tell children to draw a picture of one of the animals in the story. Have them share their pictures with the class. Have children use describing words to tell what the animal looks like and how it moves.

Remind them to speak clearly and use complete sentences as they describe their pictures. Then have children tell which words are describing words.

Comprehension

Kindergarten, Unit 2: Show and Tell

Name _____

Identify Sources

1.

2.

Directions Have children circle the best place to answer questions about what families do together. Have them identify what kinds of sources or people they could use. Then have children draw one source or person they would use. Have children take turns explaining their choices by speaking clearly and in complete sentences.

Research

59

Kindergarten, Unit 2: Show and Tell

Name _____

Adjectives for Color

purple   red   brown

1. Look at the _____ wagon.

2. I have a pair of _____ mittens.

3. It is a _____ coat.

4. _____

Directions Discuss the pictures with children and read each sentence frame aloud. Have children complete each sentence frame by writing a color word from the box on the line.

Then have children write a complete sentence using a color word to describe something. Have them share their sentences with the class.

60

Name _____

to

1. I like _____ .

2. I like _____ .

3. We like _____  .

Have children read the word in the box and name each picture. Then have them write the word *to* to complete each sentence. Have children read the completed sentences aloud.

Have children point to and say the names of letters they recognize on the page. Then have children clap once for each word as they read the sentences aloud again. Have children say other sentences with the word *to*.

Words to Know

Kindergarten, Unit 2: Show and Tell

1.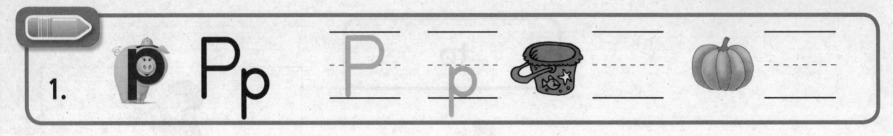

2.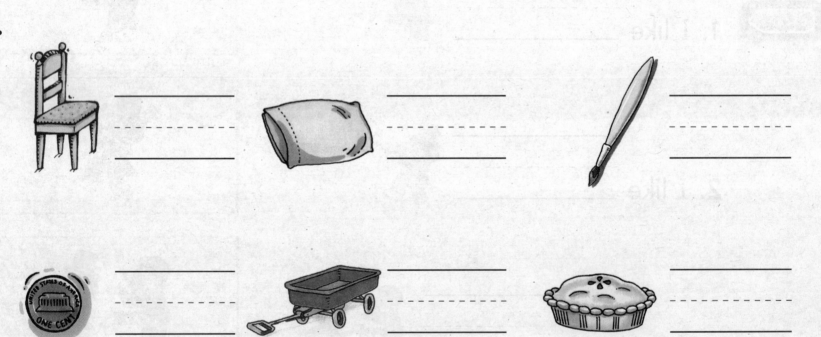

Directions Have children name the Alphafriend and its letter. Have them trace and write *P* and *p*. Then have them write *Pp* next to the pictures whose names start with the /p/ sound.

Help children think of groups of words that begin with the /p/ sound. For example, *puppy, pillow, package*.

Name _____

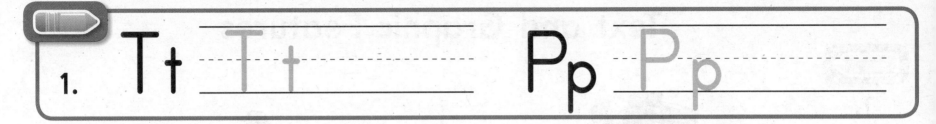

1.

2.

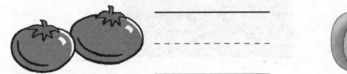 _____

 _____

 _____

 _____

 _____

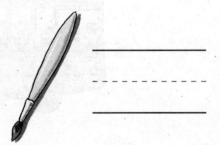 _____

Directions Have children name each letter. Have them write *Tt* and *Pp.* Then tell children to name the pictures and write the letter for the sound they hear at the beginning of each name.

Remind children to write the upper- and lowercase letters so they can be easily read, using a left-to-right and top-to-bottom progression.

Phonics

63

Kindergarten, Unit 2: Show and Tell

Name _____

Text and Graphic Features

1.

2.

Directions Tell children to look at the first set of pictures. Have them circle the picture that best shows wheels helping people to win a race. Then have them look at the second set of pictures and circle the picture that best shows wheels helping people get from place to place. Discuss with children how pictures can help them better understand information they read about. Then have children use action words, such as *roll, whiz, spin,* to describe how wheels move. Have them tell which words are action words.

Comprehension

Kindergarten, Unit 2: Show and Tell

Name _____

Gather and Record Information

Directions Page through *What Do Wheels Do All Day?* and "Wheels Long Ago and Today." Discuss with children where they might find how many wheels are on a bicycle.

Turn to page 35 of "Wheels Long Ago and Today." Help children gather information about bicycles by reading the text and asking questions about the photo. Have children record the information they find using words and illustrations.

Adjectives for Numbers

seven   two   five

1.  The bike has _____ wheels.

2.  The _____ ducks swim.

3.  There are _____ hats.

4. _____

Directions Discuss the pictures with children and read each sentence frame aloud. Have children complete each sentence frame by writing a word from the box on the line.

Then have children write a complete sentence using one of the number words. Have them share their sentences with the class.

Name _____

| see | we | a | to |

1. I _____ a  .

2. I see _____  .

3. _____ see a  .

4. We like _____  .

Directions Have children read the words in the box and name each picture. Then have them write the word *see*, *we*, *a*, or *to* to complete each sentence. Guide children to capitalize *we* at the beginning of the third sentence. Have children read the completed sentences aloud. Then have children tell a story using all of the Words to Know.

Words to Know

67

Kindergarten, Unit 2: Show and Tell

Name _____

My Idea

My Idea

Directions Help children **generate ideas** for their writing. Have children write ideas for two descriptions under *My Ideas*.

Guide children to draw pictures of the things they are thinking of writing about. Remind them to include details about their size and shape.

Name _____

1. Aa Aa Cc Cc Tt Tt Pp Pp

2.

 _____

 _____

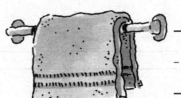 _____

 _____

 _____

 _____

Directions Have children name each letter. Have them write *Aa, Cc, Tt,* and *Pp*. Then tell children to name the pictures and write the letter for the sound they hear at the beginning of each picture name.

Remind children to write the upper- and lowercase letters so they can be easily read, using a left-to-right and top-to-bottom progression.

Name _____

My Description

Directions Help children **develop drafts** of their writing. Encourage children to use their ideas on Practice Book page 68 as a guide in writing drafts of their descriptions. Remind children that they will have a chance to add more details to their descriptions later on in the writing process. Have children use what they know about letters and words to write their descriptions. Remind them to think about words that tell about size and shape.

Writing
Kindergarten, Unit 2: Show and Tell

Name _____

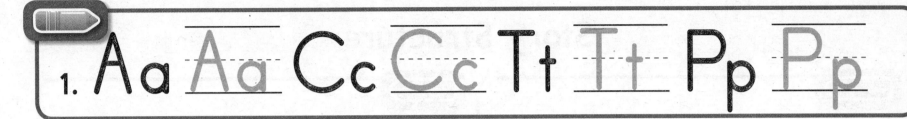

1. Aa Aa Cc Cc Tt Tt Pp Pp

2.

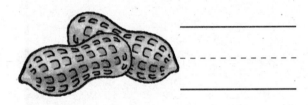 _____

 _____

 _____

 _____

 _____

 _____

Directions Have children name each letter. Have them write *Aa, Cc, Tt,* and *Pp*. Then tell children to name the pictures and write the letter for the sound they hear at the beginning of each picture name. Remind children to write the upper- and lowercase letters so they can be easily read, using a left-to-right and top-to-bottom progression.

Phonics

71

Kindergarten, Unit 2: Show and Tell

Name _____

Story Structure

Directions Discuss with children who the story is about and where it takes place. Then have them draw a picture of something that happens at the beginning of the story and at the end of the story. Have children share their pictures.

Have them use location words, such as *above, below,* or *next to* to describe parts of their pictures. Then have children sort the shapes at the top of the page into categories. Have them color the circles red, the squares yellow, and the triangles blue.

Comprehension

Kindergarten, Unit 2: Show and Tell

Name _____

My Description

Directions Help children **revise drafts** of their writing. Help children read the descriptions they wrote on Practice Book page 70. Talk about sentences and details they could add to make their descriptions even better.

Help children make changes and write their revised descriptions on the lines above.

Writing
© Houghton Mifflin Harcourt Publishing Company. All rights reserved.

Kindergarten, Unit 2: Show and Tell

Name _____

My Description

Directions Help children **edit drafts** of their writing. Help children read the descriptions they wrote on Practice Book page 73. Have them edit their drafts by writing their description again on the lines above. Remind them to leave spaces between letters and words and to write using complete sentences. Remind them to capitalize the first letter of every sentence and end every sentence with the correct punctuation. Have children consult a picture dictionary, if necessary, for correct spelling.

Writing
© Houghton Mifflin Harcourt Publishing Company. All rights reserved.

74

Kindergarten, Unit 2: Show and Tell

Name _____

Gather and Record Information

Directions Discuss with children where they might find how many sides are on a square.

Help children gather information about squares by asking questions. Have children record the information they find using words and illustrations.

Research

Kindergarten, Unit 2: Show and Tell

Name _____

Adjectives for Size and Shape

| round long small |

1. My dog has _____ ears.

2. We sit on a _____ rug.

3. The _____ mouse eats cheese.

4. _____

Directions Discuss the pictures with children and read each sentence frame aloud. Have children complete each sentence frame by writing a word from the box on the line. Have them circle the word that tells about shape and underline the words that tell about size. Then have children write a complete sentence using one of the size or shape words. Have them share their sentences with the class.

Name _____

My Description

Directions Help children **share** their writing. Have them write the final drafts of their descriptions on the lines above. Children might want to draw pictures showing the thing they chose to describe on a separate sheet of paper.

Have children take turns reading aloud their descriptions to the class and sharing their pictures. Remind them to listen attentively while others are speaking and to speak audibly and clearly when sharing their own descriptions.

Writing
© Houghton Mifflin Harcourt Publishing Company. All rights reserved.

77

Kindergarten, Unit 2: Show and Tell

_____

- -

Name _____

come   me

1. I see Sam.

_____

- - - - - - - - - - - - - - -

2. Come to _____, Sam.

_____

- - - - - - - - - - - - - - -

3. _____ to me, Sam.

_____

- - - - - - - - - - - - - - -

4. See Sam _____!

Directions Have children read the words in the box and look at each picture. Then have them write the word *come* or *me* to complete each sentence. Guide children to capitalize *come* at the beginning of the third sentence. Then have children read the sentences aloud. Have children point to and say the names of letters they recognize on the page. Then have children identify the action verb. Have children say other sentences with the words *come* and *me*.

Words to Know

78

Kindergarten, Unit 3: Outside My Door

Name _____

1.   Aa

2.

 _____

 _____

 _____

 _____

 _____

 _____

Directions Have children write their name at the top of the page. Have them name the Alphafriend and its letter. Then have children write *Aa*.

Tell children to name each picture and write the letter *Aa* when they hear the short *a* sound in the word. Remind children to write the upper- and lowercase letters so they can be easily read, using a left-to-right and top-to-bottom progression.

Name _____

Words with *a*

1.

cap　　sat

2.

mat　　Pam

3.

tap　　cat

4.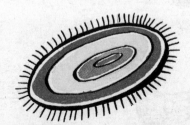

mat　　pat

Directions Tell children to look at the first picture. Then have them circle the word that matches the picture. Repeat with the rest of the pictures and words.

Have children say the words that match each picture. Then have them think of words that rhyme with each one.

Name _____

Compare and Contrast

1. I can  .

3.

2. I can

Directions Read the sentences aloud with children and discuss how the two pictures are alike and different. Then have children draw a picture to show something they like to do in the summer or winter. Have them share their pictures.

Ask them to name the setting of their pictures and use location words, such as *above* or *below*, to describe parts of their pictures. Then have them tell which words are location words.

Comprehension

Kindergarten, Unit 3: Outside My Door

Record and Publish Information

Directions Page through *Jump into January* and "Holidays All Year Long." Discuss with children where they might find more information about the month of July. Have children document their research with words and illustrations. Have them publish their research by writing and sharing a complete sentence with the class.

Research
© Houghton Mifflin Harcourt Publishing Company. All rights reserved.

82

Kindergarten, Unit 3: Outside My Door

Sentence Parts: Subject

1.  The dog chews a bone.

2. Sara sleeps.

3.  The children like to slide.

4. _____

- -

_____

Directions Discuss the pictures with children and read each sentence aloud. Have children underline the naming part, or subject, in each sentence.

Then have children write a complete sentence. Have them share their sentences with the class. Challenge the class to identify the subject in each sentence.

Name _____

with   my

1. See _____ cat.

2. See my cat _____ a can.

3. See my cat _____ a mat.

4. See _____ cat.

Directions Have children read the words in the box and look at each picture. Then have them write the word *with* or *my* to complete each sentence. Have children read the completed sentences aloud.

Have children point to and say the names of the letters they recognize on the page. Then have children clap once for each word as they read the sentences aloud again. Have children say other sentences with the words *with* and *my*.

Name _____

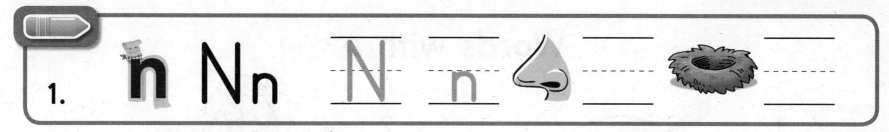

1.

2.

Directions Have children write their name at the top of the page. Have them name the Alphafriend and its letter. Then have children trace and write *N* and *n*.

Have children write *Nn* next to the pictures whose names start with the /n/ sound. Help children think of groups of words that begin with the /n/ sound. For example, *Nan knits nightly.*

Name _____

Words with *n*

1.

_____ a n

2.

_____ a p

3.

m a _____

4.

c _____ n

Directions Tell children to look at the first picture and name it. Then have them write the missing letter to complete the picture's name. Repeat with the rest of the pictures and words.

Say pairs of rhyming and non-rhyming words that go with each picture. Have children raise their hand when they hear a pair of words that rhyme.

Name _____

Conclusions

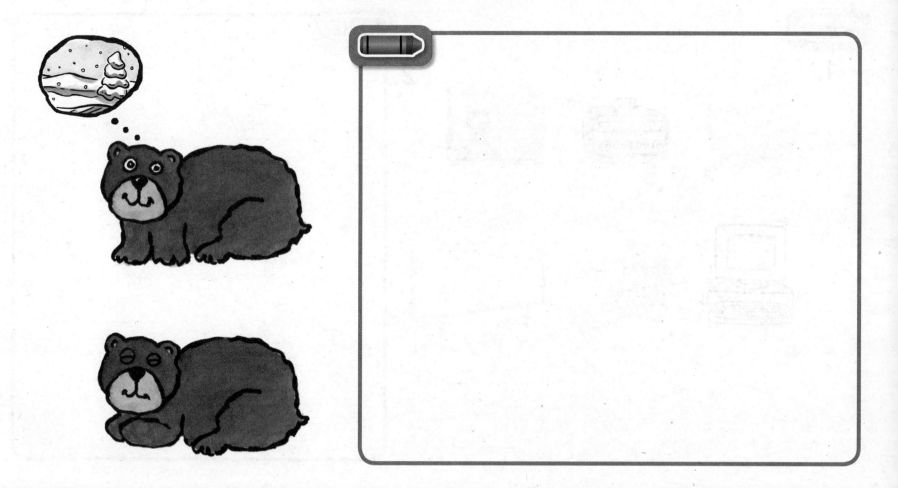

Directions Have children look at the pictures and remind them what happened at the beginning of the story. Then have children illustrate how the bear feels when he hears the snow is coming. Have children share their pictures with the class. Have them use location words, such as *on* or *in* to describe their pictures. Have them identify these words as location words. Discuss with children how they used what they already knew and what they learned from the story when they drew their pictures.

Name _____

Identify Media Forms

1.

2.

Directions Page through "How Water Changes" with children. Then have them identify and discuss the different forms of media above. Have children circle which forms they think might help them better understand the different states of water. Then have children choose the best media form for understanding water and draw a picture of it. Have children take turns explaining their choice by speaking one at a time and in complete sentences.

Media Literacy

Kindergarten, Unit 3: Outside My Door

Name _____

Sentence Parts: Verb

1.  The mouse rides a bike.

2.  Josh builds a snowman.

3.  The cat naps.

4. _____

Lesson 13
PRACTICE BOOK

What Color is Nature?
Words to Know: *you, what*

Name _____

you   what

_____

1. _____ come with me.

_____

2. _____ can we see?

_____

3. We can see _____ and me!

Words to Know

Kindergarten, Unit 3: Outside My Door

Name _____

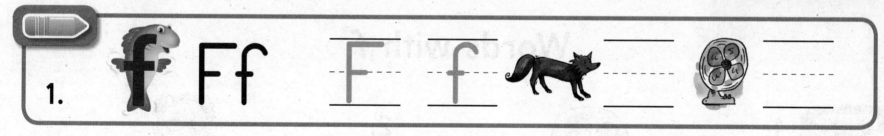

1.

2.

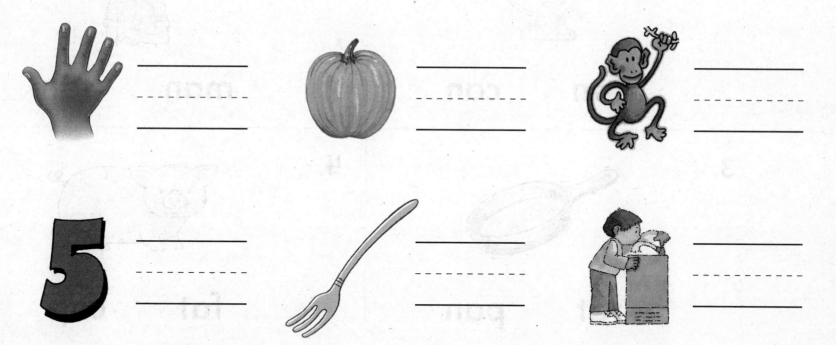

Directions Have children write their name at the top of the page. Have them name the Alphafriend and its letter. Then have children trace and write *F* and *f*.

Have children write *Ff* next to the pictures whose names begin with the /f/ sound. Help children think of groups of words that begin with the /f/ sound. For example, *Four frogs fell far*.

Phonics

91

Kindergarten, Unit 3: Outside My Door

Name _____

Words with *f*

1.

fan   can

2.

man   fan

3.

fat   pan

4.

fat   cap

Directions Tell children to look at the first picture. Then have them circle the word that matches the picture. Repeat with the rest of the pictures and words.

Have children say the words that match each picture. Then have them think of words that rhyme with each one.

Name _____

Author's Purpose

Directions Tell children to look at the pictures in the boxes and identify each one. Read the following sentence starter aloud and model how to complete it for box 1: *The author wanted me to know about___*. Have children write the response on the line below the first box. Help children complete the sentence for each remaining box. Then have children sort the pictures into categories by drawing a circle around the items that have bright colors.

Comprehension

93

Kindergarten, Unit 3: Outside My Door

Name _____

Ask Questions

Directions Have children share questions they might have about *What Color Is Nature?* Encourage them to discuss the different colors in nature. Remind children to speak in complete sentences.

Have children draw a picture of their favorite thing from nature from the selection. Have children take turns explaining their choice by speaking clearly and in complete sentences.

Research

Kindergarten, Unit 3: Outside My Door

Name _____

Complete Sentences

1. we see a red rose

2. the brown dog

3. _____

4. _____

Directions Read aloud the page with children. Have children circle the happy face if the words are a complete sentence and the sad face if they are not. Then help children make each sentence complete. As children rewrite each sentence, have them capitalize the first letter in the sentence and put a period at the end.

Grammar

Kindergarten, Unit 3: Outside My Door

Name _____

are   now

_____
1. _____ you Sam?

_____
2. You _____ Nat.

_____
3. _____ you Sam?

_____
4. _____ I see you, Sam!

Directions Have children read the words in the box and look at each picture. Then have them write the word *are* or *now* to complete each sentence. Guide children to capitalize the first letter at the beginning of a sentence. Then have children read the sentences aloud. Have children point to and say the names of the letters they recognize on the page. Then have children clap once for each word as they read the sentences aloud again. Have children say other sentences with the words *are* and *now*.

Words to Know

96

Kindergarten, Unit 3: Outside My Door

Name _____

1.  Bb

2.

 _____

 _____

 _____

 _____

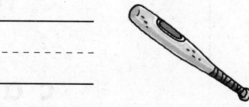 _____

 _____

Directions Have children write their name at the top of the page. Have them name the Alphafriend and its letter. Then have children trace and write *B* and *b*.

Have children write *Bb* next to the pictures whose names begin with the /b/ sound. Help children think of groups of words that begin with the /b/ sound. For example, *Busy blue birds blink.*

Phonics

97

Kindergarten, Unit 3: Outside My Door

Name _____

Words with *b*

1.

___ a t

2.

___ a t

3.

m ___ n

4.

c a ___

Directions Tell children to look at the first picture and name it. Then have them write the missing letter to complete the picture's name. Repeat with the rest of the pictures and words.

Have children circle the words with *b*. Say pairs of rhyming and non-rhyming words that go with each picture. Have children raise their hand when they hear a pair of words that rhyme.

Phonics

Kindergarten, Unit 3: Outside My Door

Name

Cause and Effect

Cause

Effect

Directions Have children look at the picture and discuss what is happening. Then have them draw a picture of the effect it has in the story. Have children share their pictures with the class and tell about the key event in their pictures. Then have them identify a character from the story and describe the character's actions using action words they know. Have children identify them as action words.

Comprehension

99

Kindergarten, Unit 3: Outside My Door

Name _____

Identify Sources

1.

2.

Directions Have children circle the best place to find information about animals that live around a pond. Have them identify what kinds of sources or people they could use.

Then have children draw one source or person they would use. Have children take turns explaining their choice by speaking clearly and in complete sentences.

Name _____

Action Verbs in Past Tense

I We

1. _____

_____

2. _____

_____

Directions Have children name each picture. Then have them complete each sentence by writing a word from the box and circling the picture that shows what happened in the past.

Have children read their sentences aloud using a past-tense verb to describe the picture they circled. Tell them to speak clearly as they share their sentences and to listen carefully to others as they share.

Name _____

now   what   with   you

1. _____ can you see?

2. I can see Pam _____ a bat.

3. _____ Pam can bat.

4. Bam! _____ can see Pam bat.

Directions Have children read <u>the words</u> in the box and look at each picture. Then have them write the correct word from the box to complete each sentence. Guide children to capitalize the first letter at the beginning of a sentence. Then have children read the sentences aloud. Have children point to and say the names of letters they recognize on the page. Then have them clap once for each word as they read the sentences aloud again. Have children tell a story using all of the Words to Know.

Name _____

My Ideas

Directions Help children discuss and **generate ideas** for their writing. Have children write ideas for their stories under *My Ideas*. Guide children to write words or draw pictures showing the characters, setting, and what will happen in their stories.

Writing

Kindergarten, Unit 3: Outside My Door

Name _____

1. Aa Aa Ff Ff Nn Nn Bb Bb

2.

 _____

 _____

 _____

 _____

 _____

 _____

Directions Have children write their name at the top of the page. Have them name each letter. Then have them trace *Aa, Ff, Nn,* and *Bb*.

Tell children to name the pictures and write the letter for the sound they hear at the beginning of each name. Remind children to write the upper- and lowercase letters so they can be easily read, using a left-to-right and top-to-bottom progression.

Name _____

My Story

Directions Help children **develop drafts** of their writing. Encourage them to use their ideas on Practice Book page 103 as a guide. Have children use what they know about letters and words to write their stories.

Remind them to think about events in their stories and the order in which they happen. Have children begin sequencing details and actions in their stories.

Writing

Kindergarten, Unit 3: Outside My Door

Review Words with *a, n, f, b*

1.

cab   can

2.

pan   sat

3.

cat   bat

4.

fan   man

Directions Tell children to look at the first picture. Then have them circle the word that matches the picture. Repeat with the rest of the pictures and words.

Have children say the words that match each picture. Then have them think of words that rhyme with each one.

Name _____

Sequence of Events

Directions Have children look at the pictures. Discuss what the author tells about at the beginning of the selection. Then have children draw a picture of what the author tells about at the end of the selection. Have children share their pictures.

Have them use sequence words, such as *first, next,* and *last,* to retell the selection in the order in which the author tells about the sky. Then have children tell which words are sequence words.

Comprehension

Kindergarten, Unit 3: Outside My Door

Name _____

My Story

Directions Help children **revise drafts** of their writing. Help them read the stories they wrote on Practice Book page 105. Talk about sentences and details they could add to make their stories even better.

Help children organize their story by beginning, middle, and end. Have them write their revised stories on the lines above.

Writing

Kindergarten, Unit 3: Outside My Door

Name _____

My Story

Directions Help children **edit drafts** of their writing. Help children read the stories they wrote on Practice Book page 108. Have them edit their drafts by writing their stories again on the lines above. Remind them to leave spaces between letters and words and to write using complete sentences. Remind them to capitalize the first letter of every sentence and end every sentence with the correct punctuation. Have children consult a picture dictionary, if necessary, for correct spelling.

Writing

Kindergarten, Unit 3: Outside My Door

Name _____

Gather and Record Information

Directions Discuss with children where they might find out what things are in the sky at night.

Have children gather information about the night sky by asking questions. Have children record the information they find using words and illustrations.

Statements

1. the moon and stars

2. we see an airplane

3.  _____

4.  _____

Directions Read each statement aloud with children. Have children circle the happy face if the statement is complete and the sad face if it is not.

Then help children rewrite each statement correctly. Have them change the beginning letter of the first word to a capital letter and add a period to the end. Have children read the statements aloud.

Name _____

My Story

Directions Help children **share** their writing. Have them write the final drafts of their stories on the lines above. Children might want to draw pictures to illustrate their stories on separate sheets of paper. Have children take turns reading aloud their stories to the class and sharing their pictures. Have them identify and use sequence words such as *first, next,* and *last*. Remind children to listen attentively while others are speaking and to speak audibly and clearly when sharing their own stories.

Writing

Kindergarten, Unit 3: Outside My Door

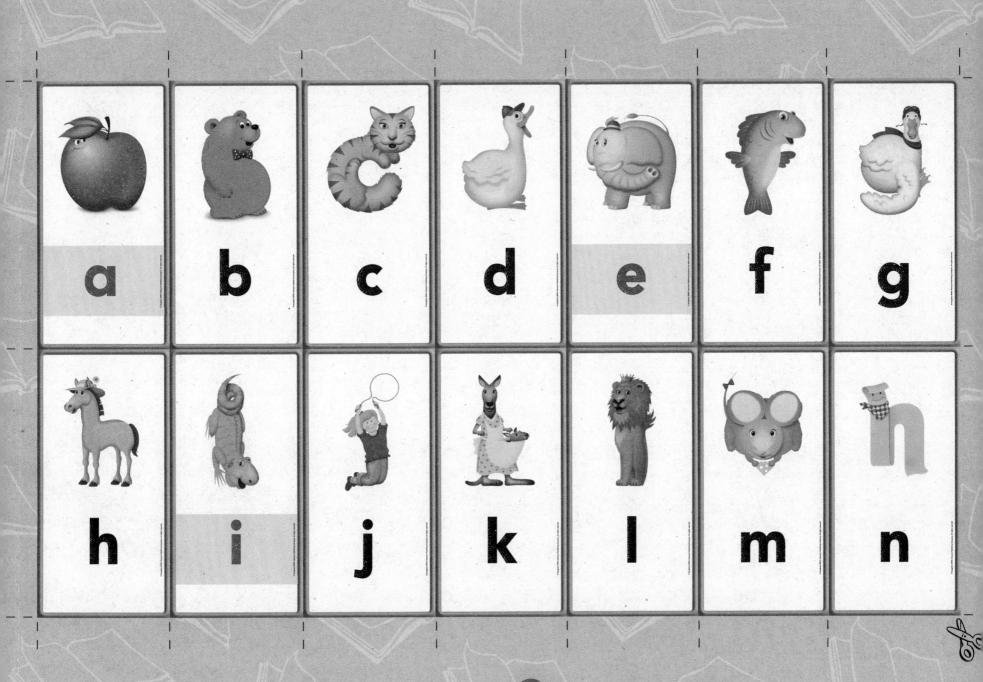

a
b
c
d
e
f
g

h
i
j
k
l
m
n

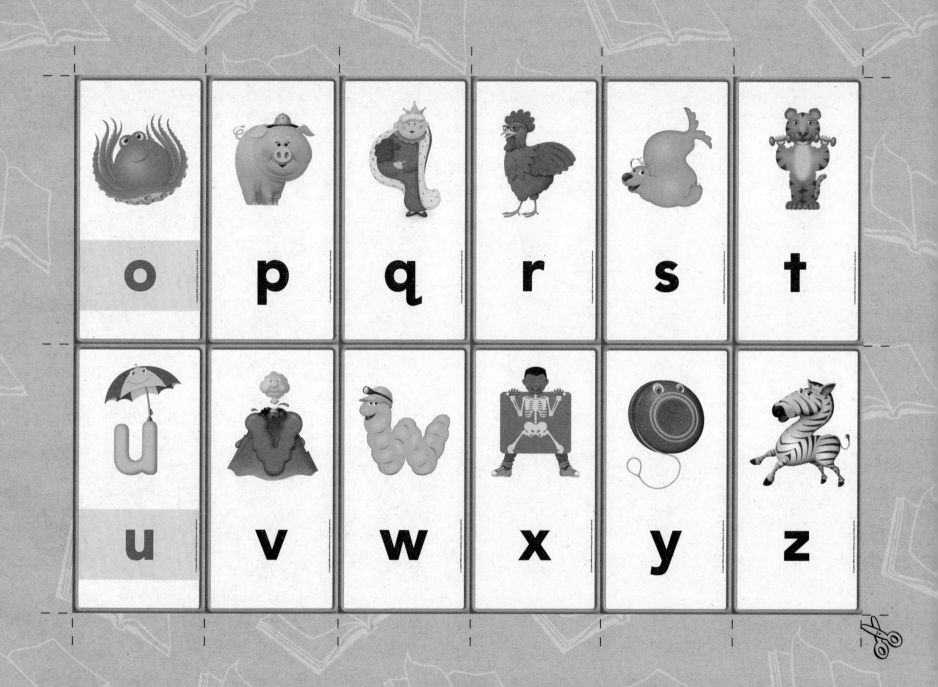

o p q r s t

u v w x y z

A A A B B C C D D

E E E F F G G H H

I I J J K K L L M

M N N O O P P Q Q

R R S S T T U U V

V W W X X Y Y Z Z

d	d	c	c	b	b	a	a	a
h	h	g	g	f	f	e	e	e
m	l	l	k	k	j	j	i	i
q	q	p	p	p	o	o	n	n	m
v	u	u	t	t	s	s	r	r
z	z	y	y	x	x	w	w	v

see	I
we	like
a	the
to	and

you	come
what	me
are	with
now	my